Mark, Mel, Jeff, Jazz and Alex all support the Sunsets Rockets team.

At matches they unroll a banner with 'Sunset Rockets' on it.

Today they are near to the football pitch ...

... They see a gap in the door and go in! On the pitch are The Sunset Rockets!

SUNSET ROCKET

But they are seen by Coach Reed. He yells at them!

He is really upset and chucks them off the pitch.

You lot ... off you go! Now!

The Rockets moan. They think he is so unfair. But in the car park they get a real shock!

They rush to stop the thugs kicking Coach Reed's car, and call the cops.

The thugs are kicking the car!
Get the cops!
POL

Coach Reed is harsh with the thugs.
Lock them up!
The police put them in the police car.

Then the coach turns to the Rockets.

They think he is still upset with them, but they follow him.

Hey, Rockets! Meet my new pals!
But in the room are the Sunset Rockets! Cool!